LINCOLNWOOD PUBLIC LIBRARY

3 1242 00101 3110

W9-BLY-822

LINCOLNWOOD LIBRARY
4000 West Pratt Avenue
Lincolnwood, IL 60646

BASEBALL LEGENDS

Hank Aaron
Grover Cleveland Alexander
Ernie Banks
Johnny Bench
Yogi Berra
Roy Campanella
Roberto Clemente
Ty Cobb
Dizzy Dean
Joe DiMaggio
Bob Feller
Jimmie Foxx
Lou Gehrig
Bob Gibson
Rogers Hornsby
Walter Johnson
Sandy Koufax
Mickey Mantle
Christy Mathewson
Willie Mays
Stan Musial
Satchel Paige
Brooks Robinson
Frank Robinson
Jackie Robinson
Babe Ruth
Duke Snider
Warren Spahn
Willie Stargell
Honus Wagner
Ted Williams
Carl Yastrzemski
Cy Young

CHELSEA HOUSE PUBLISHERS

MAR 11 1993

BASEBALL LEGENDS

HANK AARON

Jim Tackach

Introduction by
Jim Murray

Senior Consultant
Earl Weaver

LINCOLNWOOD LIBRARY

CHELSEA HOUSE PUBLISHERS
New York • Philadelphia

Produced by James Charlton Associates
New York, New York.

Designed by Hudson Studio
Ossining, New York.

Typesetting by LinoGraphics
New York, New York.

Picture research by Carolann Hawkins
Cover illustration by Dan O'Leary

Copyright © 1992 by Chelsea House Publishers, a division of Main
Line Book Co. All rights reserved. Printed and bound in the United
States of America.

3 5 7 9 8 6 4 2

Library of Congress Cataloging-in-Publication Data

Tackach, James.
    Hank Aaron/James Tackach; introduction by Jim Murray; senior
consultant, Earl Weaver.
    p. cm.—(Baseball legends)
    Includes bibliographical references and index.
    Summary: A biography of Hall of Fame baseball player Hank
Aaron, who broke Babe Ruth's career home run record.
    ISBN 0-7910-1165-8.—ISBN 0-7910-1199-2 (ppk.)
    1. Aaron, Hank, 1934- —Juvenile literature. 2. Baseball
players—United States—Biography—Juvenile literature. [1. Aaron,
Hank, 1934- . 2. Afro-Americans—Biography.] I. Title.
II. Series.
GV865.A25T33 1991   91-525
796.357'092—dc20   CIP
    [B]   AC

CONTENTS

WHAT MAKES A STAR

Jim Murray

No one has ever been able to explain to me the mysterious alchemy that makes one man a .350 hitter and another player, more or less identical in physical makeup, hard put to hit .200. You look at an Al Kaline, who played with the Detroit Tigers from 1953 to 1974. He was pale, stringy, almost poetic-looking. He always seemed to be struggling against a bad case of mononucleosis. But with a bat in his hands, he was King Kong. During his career, he hit 399 home runs, rapped out 3,007 hits, and compiled a .297 batting average.

Form isn't the reason. The first time anybody saw Roberto Clemente step into the batter's box for the Pittsburgh Pirates, the best guess was that Clemente would be back in Double A ball in a week. He had one foot in the bucket and held his bat at an awkward angle—he looked as though he couldn't hit an outside pitch. A lot of other ballplayers may have had a better-looking stance. Yet they never led the National League in hitting in four different years, the way Clemente did.

Not every ballplayer is born with the ability to hit a curveball. Nor is exceptional hand-eye coordination the key to heavy hitting. Big-league locker rooms are filled with players who have all the attributes, save one: discipline. Every baseball man can tell you a story about a pitcher who throws a ball faster than anyone has ever seen but who has no control on or *off* the field.

The Hall of Fame is full of people who transformed themselves into great ballplayers by working at the sport, by studying the game, and making sacrifices. They're overachievers—and winners. If you want to find them, just watch the World Series. Or simply read about New York Yankee great Lou Gehrig; Ted Williams, "the Splendid Splinter" of the Boston Red Sox; or the Dodgers' strikeout king Sandy Koufax.

A pitcher *should* be able to win a lot of ballgames with a 98-miles-per-hour fastball. But what about the pitcher who wins 20 games a year with a fastball so slow that you can catch it with your teeth? Bob Feller of the Cleveland Indians got into the Hall of Fame with a blazing fastball that glowed in the dark. National League star Grover Cleveland Alexander got there with a pitch that took considerably longer to reach the plate; but when it did arrive, the pitch was exactly where Alexander wanted it to be—and the last place the batter expected it to be.

There are probably more players with exceptional ability who didn't make it to the major leagues than there are who did. A number of great hitters, bored with fielding practice, had to be dropped from their team because their home-run production didn't make up for their lapses in the field. And then there are players like Brooks Robinson of the Baltimore Orioles, who made himself into a human vacuum cleaner at third base because he knew that working hard to become an expert fielder would win him a job in the big leagues.

A star is not something that flashes through the sky. That's a comet. Or a meteor. A star is something you can steer ships by. It stays in place and gives off a steady glow; it is fixed, permanent. A star works at being a star.

And that's how you tell a star in baseball. He shows up night after night and takes pride in how brightly he shines. He's Willie Mays running so hard his hat keeps falling off; Ty Cobb sliding to stretch a single into a double; Lou Gehrig, after being fooled in his first two at-bats, belting the next pitch off the light tower because he's taken the time to study the pitcher. Stars never take themselves for granted. That's why they're stars.

NUMBER 715

For more than half a century, Babe Ruth had been baseball's career home-run leader. His lifetime total of homers had stood at 714 since May 25, 1935, when the Babe, playing for the Boston Braves, smacked three four-baggers against the Pittsburgh Pirates at Forbes Field. Following Ruth's retirement a few days later, many great sluggers—Jimmie Foxx, Ted Williams, Mickey Mantle, Willie Mays—had taken a shot at his record. But all had fallen considerably short. Mays had come the closest, with 660.

By Opening Day of the 1974 season, it was clear that Ruth's record was doomed. Hank Aaron, a veteran of 20 seasons with the Milwaukee and Atlanta Braves, was within two home runs of placing his name above Ruth's on the all-time list. He had racked up 40 homers during the 1973 season, bringing his total to 713. No one doubted that Aaron would erase Babe's mark in the early weeks of the new season.

Aaron went about his business quickly and efficiently. In the Braves' opening game at Riverfront Stadium in Cincinnati, in his first at bat, he hammered a 3–1 pitch from the Reds'

At the press conference after the game in which he hit his historic 715th career home run, a happy Aaron fields questions from one of the nearly 300 reporters assembled there.

Jack Billingham into the left-field seats. With his first swing of the season, Aaron had tied Ruth.

Four days later, on April 8, a cool and cloudy Monday evening, a crowd of reporters and celebrities arrived at Atlanta-Fulton County Stadium hoping to see Hammerin' Hank set the record. An extra press box had been constructed along the right-field line to help seat all the reporters. Entertainers Sammy Davis, Jr., and Pearl Bailey were on hand, and an audience of 35 million was watching the nationally televised game. The pregame ceremonies featured exploding cannons and the release of hundreds of helium-filled balloons. A huge American flag had been painted on the outfield grass.

When Aaron was asked to say a few words to the big crowd before the game, he was characteristically modest and soft-spoken. "I just want to thank all my friends for being here," he said. "I'm just hoping this thing will get over with tonight."

Veteran Al Downing started the game for the visiting Los Angeles Dodgers. A former Yankees ace, he had pitched in two World Series with the New Yorkers. Ten years earlier, he had led the American League in strikeouts, and in 1971 he had won 20 games for the Dodgers. Now nearing the end of an admirable pitching career, he was not looking to become Aaron's 715th victim.

In the first inning, Downing worked Aaron carefully, throwing breaking balls at the corners of the plate. He walked Aaron on five pitches; Hank did not swing at any of them. When Downing threw ball four and Aaron trotted to first base, the fans booed in disapproval. They had paid to see their hero swing the bat.

Aaron came up again in the 4th inning with one runner on base. Again Downing pitched cautiously, missing the plate with his first offering. On the next pitch, his catcher signaled for a fastball. Downing's fastball, once overpowering, was now really a hard sinker. This pitch, however, did not sink, and Aaron crushed it on a line toward the Atlanta bullpen behind left-center field. Dodger left fielder Bill Buckner raced to the fence and tried to scale it as he saw the ball go sailing beyond his reach. Meanwhile, the Braves in the bullpen scrambled to position themselves to catch the ball, which easily cleared the fence and settled into the glove of relief pitcher Tom House.

Immediately, the crowd of 52,780 people was on its feet and cheering. So was Jimmy Wynn, one of the Dodger outfielders, who dropped his glove and began to clap. As Aaron rounded the bases, all the Dodger infielders extended their

Aaron connects with one of the specially marked balls and drives it for his 715th career homer. After home run number 700, the Braves supplied umpires with balls marked with infrared code numbers. When Aaron came to the plate, the regular ball was removed and the umpire would put a marked ball in the game. If Aaron hit a homer, and a fan returned the ball, the Braves would know if it was the actual home-run ball.

Hank's parents, Herbert and Estella Aaron, celebrate as Aaron circles the bases after hitting his historic 715th home run. Herbert Aaron had thrown out the first ball to start the game.

hands to offer congratulations. By the time Aaron reached home plate, his teammates were waiting there to shake his hand and slap his back. His mother and wife climbed down from their box seats to embrace the new home-run king. The game had to be held up for more than 10 minutes while dignitaries and friends congratulated the man who had just hit the historic homer. But when someone handed Aaron a microphone, all he could say was, "Thank you. Thank you... thank you," he repeated. "I just thank God it's all over."

Shortly after the game continued, President Richard M. Nixon telephoned the ballpark to speak with Aaron, but he was informed that Aaron could not come to the phone right then because he was busy playing the outfield. Aaron did find time to return the call between innings, however. "It was a long struggle," he told the president, "but I finally made it."

Aaron's achievement was, indeed, the end of a long struggle. But that record-breaking homer on April 8, 1974, was only one of many highlights in Henry Aaron's long and splendid career. The man who erased Babe Ruth's home-run mark was more than a slugger; he was a complete player who excelled at every aspect of the game: hitting, fielding, and baserunning. Even if Hank Aaron had not hit 715 home runs, his story would still be worth telling.

2

AN ALABAMA BOYHOOD

On February 5, 1934, the day before Babe Ruth's 39th birthday, Estella Aaron gave birth to her third child, Henry Louis Aaron. Herbert Aaron, the boy's father, was a boilermaker's helper with the Alabama Drydock and Ship-building Company in Mobile, Alabama. Henry was born during hard times—in the middle of the Great Depression—and his father was happy to be bringing home $75 or $80 a week to support his family.

Estella Aaron claims that Henry (he was not called "Hank" until he began playing professional baseball) was an easy child to raise. He stayed out of trouble because he was constantly playing baseball. Even at age four, he could be found at the nearest ball field with the neighborhood's older boys, an oversized glove dangling from his small left hand. Baseball equipment was not

Mobile, Alabama, in the mid-1940s, when Aaron was growing up. Two other future Hall of Famers, Billy Williams and Willie McCovey, each four years younger than Aaron, also grew up in Mobile.

easily acquired by youngsters during the Depression, so Henry practiced in his yard with a ball of tightly wound rags. When he finally got hold of a rubber ball, he used one of his mother's broomsticks to smack it against the side of his house.

During the 1930s, the Alabama public schools were racially segregated; white youngsters attended one school, while black children attended another. After grammar school, Henry attended Mobile's Central High School. Unfortunately, Central High did not have a baseball team, but Henry did join its fast-pitch softball team. In his spare time, he played baseball for the Pritchett Athletics, a local sandlot team.

As talented as he was, Henry Aaron dared not dream for very long about playing big-league baseball. At the time, the major leagues, by a longstanding agreement among team owners, were reserved for white players only. Talented blacks such as Josh Gibson, Ray Dandridge, and Biz Mackey played either in the Negro Leagues or on "barnstorming" teams that traveled around the country, competing against local clubs for a few dollars per game.

All that changed in 1945, when Branch Rickey, president of the Brooklyn Dodgers, signed Jackie Robinson to play for his Montreal farm team. Two years later, Robinson was brought up to the majors, and soon other black players— Roy Campanella, Don Newcombe, Larry Doby— were signed by major-league teams.

Suddenly, a youngster like Henry Aaron could do more than just dream about a major-league baseball career. Henry followed Jackie Robinson's progress very closely. Once, Robinson's Dodgers came to Mobile to play an exhibition game against

a local team, and Henry and his father attended the event. After seeing the graceful Robinson on the baseball diamond, Henry turned to his dad and said, "I'm going to be like him. Before he's through playing, I'll be up there with him."

Herbert Aaron did nothing to discourage his son's future ambition as long as it did not interfere with his present responsibility—getting an education. One day when he was still in high school, Henry cut class and went to a poolroom to hear a Brooklyn Dodgers game broadcast on the big radio. As it turned out, Herbert Aaron had the afternoon off and just happened to walk into that very same poolhall.

"I was listening to the baseball game," Henry told his dad. "Jackie Robinson plays for Brooklyn, and I want to be a baseball player, and I'll learn more about how to play second base listen-

Central High School in Mobile, where Aaron went to school. The principal once chased him down the halls with a cane because Aaron, a star athlete, had quit the football team.

Jackie Robinson, Hank's boyhood hero, broke major league baseball's racial barrier in 1947. When Robinson came to Mobile in 1948, Aaron went to hear him speak.

ing to him play than I will in a schoolroom."

But Herbert Aaron dismissed his son's argument. "You don't think these fellows playing in the big leagues are dumb, do you?" he asked.

"No, but they didn't learn how to catch or how to hit a baseball in a classroom," Henry replied. "I've made up my mind. I want to be a baseball player."

"You can still be a baseball player," Herbert Aaron replied. "You get an education."

Henry did not cut any more classes after that. But one day, while he was playing a summer recreation-league softball game, the talented

teenager was approached by Ed Scott, who scouted players for a local semi-pro team called the Mobile Black Bears. "Aaron, how would you like to play baseball and make some money?" Scott asked him after the game.

"I'll have to ask Mama about that," Henry replied. "She doesn't want me to be playing baseball. She wants me to get an education."

"Oh, this is just once a week, son," Scott explained. "You just play on a Sunday afternoon and make a little money, that's all. It's not every kid that gets a chance to play for the Mobile Black Bears."

"I know I can't if it's Sunday," Henry said. "Mama won't let me." Sunday was a church and family day in the Aaron household.

Scott went to see the Aarons three Sundays in a row before he finally convinced them to allow Henry to play. Henry would be making $10 per game, a lot of money for a high-school student in 1950. More important, he would get a chance to develop his skills by playing against strong competition.

In the spring of 1951, the Indianapolis Clowns of the Negro American League came to Mobile to play the Black Bears. Bunny Downs, an ex–Negro Leaguer who was serving as the Clowns' traveling secretary, was impressed with Henry, who was playing shortstop at the time. After the game, Downs came over to speak with him.

"How old are you, kid?" he asked.

"Seventeen," Henry told him.

"Are you still in high school?"

"Yessir."

"When do you get out?"

"I'll graduate next year."

"Do you always play shortstop?"

Tommie Aaron, five years younger than Hank, joined his brother on the Braves in 1962 and was a teammate for seven years. In his first year, Tommie hit a career-high eight homers; three of them came in games in which Hank also homered.

"I play anywhere they want me to play."

"That's a nice attitude," Downs said. "How would you like to play for the Indianapolis Clowns?"

"I don't see any reason why not," Henry replied.

Downs said he would be back the following spring—with a contract—when Henry was 18. And almost exactly one year later, Henry received a contract in the mail offering him $200 per month to play for the Clowns.

Before he signed the contract, however, Henry had to convince his mother that he was ready to leave home. Because he would have to go away from school a month before graduation, he also had to promise her that he would return and get his high-school diploma (a promise he kept).

So, one May morning in 1952, Estella Aaron gave her son two sandwiches, two clean pairs of pants, and two dollars. Then she took him to the Mobile railroad station, where he boarded a train to the Clowns' spring training camp in Winston-Salem, North Carolina.

The train departed, and for the first time in his life Henry was on his own. Every time it stopped at a station, he thought about getting off and heading back to Mobile, but he stayed aboard until Winston-Salem. He was on his way to becoming a professional baseball player.

PLAYING WITH THE PROS

T he Indianapolis Clowns were rarely in Indianapolis. They usually trained in Winston-Salem, and they played wherever their old team bus could take them. They criss-crossed the country, playing Negro League and local teams in big cities or small towns.

During spring training, the Clowns stayed at an old hotel above a poolroom. When they took to the road, they slept in the team bus, except on Saturday nights, when they would check into a hotel for a decent night's rest. During good weather, they might play 8 or 10 games per week, and sometimes they played tripleheaders on Sundays.

When Aaron arrived at the Clowns' training camp, he was a complete unknown. He was 6 feet tall, with a shy manner and a skinny frame that made him look younger than his 18 years. Many of the Clowns did not believe that this quiet, frail-

Aaron (left, second row) poses with the 1952 Eau Claire Bears. Future major leaguers Wes Covington (top row, third from right) and Johnny Goryl (front row, second from left) were also on the team.

23

looking kid would make the club. He certainly did not look like much at the plate with his cross-handed grip. (Even though he batted righty, he held his left hand above his right on the bat.) When team jackets were given to the players, Aaron did not even get one.

The quiet youngster from Mobile did his most impressive talking on the field—with his arm, his legs, and most of all his bat. He threw hard and accurately, he ran swiftly, and he hit the ball a long way for a skinny kid. Even with his cross-handed swing, his strong wrists and forearms allowed him to whip the bat forward with incredible speed and force. The Clowns were soon calling him "Little Brother" and marveling at his abilities.

Aaron was, in fact, too good for the Clowns. By mid-June 1952, he was batting above .400. Syd Pollock, the Clowns' owner, knew he had a player talented enough to play in the big leagues one day. He figured that he could make more money by selling Aaron's contract to a major-league team than by showcasing him on the Negro Leagues circuit, especially now that the Negro League teams were playing more exhibitions than competitive games. The best black players had begun to play in the big leagues, and black fans were deserting the Negro Leagues games. Reckoning that the black leagues were probably destined to die, Pollock wrote in a short note to John Mullen, farm-team director of the Boston Braves: "We got an 18-year-old shortstop batting cleanup for us."

The Braves quickly sent scout Dewey Griggs to watch Aaron play in a doubleheader against the Kansas City Monarchs in Buffalo, New York. The New York Giants also had a scout on hand

to see Aaron.

Playing in front of Griggs, Aaron turned in one of the best performances of his young career. In the two games against Kansas City, he got 7 hits in 9 at bats, including 2 homers, one over the left-field fence and one to deep right field. At shortstop, Aaron also assisted in five double plays. Griggs was initially concerned about Aaron's throwing ability; the youngster tended to flip the ball instead of firing it to the first baseman. But in the second game, Aaron went deep into the third-base hole to snag a grounder and drilled the ball over to first with time to spare. Later, Griggs spoke to Aaron and convinced him to abandon his cross-handed batting grip.

Griggs immediately began negotiating with Pollock for Aaron's services. The Giants, who had beaten out the Braves and signed another

Aaron joined teammates Joe Adcock and Eddie Mathews in 1954, and in the next nine seasons the three sluggers slammed out 884 home runs. As the most potent home run duo in major-league history, Mathews and Aaron hit 857 in the 13 seasons they played together.

black youngster from Alabama—Willie Mays— were also after Hank, but Griggs made the deal. He offered Pollock $10,000 for Aaron—$2,500 immediately, with the rest to come as Aaron moved up in the Braves' minor-league system. He also offered Hank $50 more per month than the Giants were willing to pay, and so Henry Aaron became a Brave. Before the end of June, he was in an airplane en route to Eau Claire, Wisconsin, in the Northern League.

Aaron quickly made friends with two black teammates, Wes Covington and Julie Bowers, who were also spending their first year in the Braves' farm system. Bowers would not make it to the major leagues, but Wes Covington would join the parent Braves team two years after Aaron did. Having two black teammates helped the young Aaron, but still he was unhappy in Eau Claire. He was homesick for his family. After only a few weeks, he called home to tell his folks that he was leaving the team. Estella Aaron was

Braves manager Charlie Grimm congratulates Aaron after the rookie slugged a homer against the Boston Red Sox in a 1954 spring training game.

happy to hear that her boy would be coming home. But Henry's older brother, Herbert Jr., who was home at the time, had a different reaction.

Taking the phone from his mother, Herbert made his feelings clear. "Man, are you out of your mind?" he scolded Henry. "Don't make a fool of yourself. I just wish I'd had the chance you've got."

"Well, come on up here if you think it's so great," Henry said.

"Henry, don't make a mistake," Herbert urged. "If you come home, you're making a big mistake. I know you're homesick, but see if you can't stick it out."

Hank took his brother's advice and stayed, and he never regretted that decision. A few days later, he was named the league's shortstop in the upcoming all-star game, even though he had played in only 18 games. The honor made him feel he really did belong in professional baseball, and he went on to have a spectacular season: a .336 batting average with 9 homers and 61 RBIs in only 87 games. His teammate Wes Covington was not far behind with a .330 average and 99 runs batted in.

The next year, 1953, Aaron was sent to spring training in Kissimmee, Florida, with the Milwaukee Brewers, then the Braves' top-level farm team. The manager, Tommy Holmes, was not impressed with Aaron. Holmes, a former player with the Braves, did not like the way Aaron often hit to right field. Holmes wanted Aaron to pull the ball to left. Even after watching two of Aaron's shots clear the right-field fence in an exhibition game, Holmes was skeptical about Aaron's potential. "He'll never be a big-league player," Holmes proclaimed. "He can't pull the ball."

So Aaron was sent to Jacksonville, Florida, in the South Atlantic (Sally) League. Jacksonville manager Ben Geraghty moved Aaron from short-stop to second base. Geraghty, who took an immediate liking to the quiet youngster, warned that he might expect some trouble as the first black player in the Sally League.

Aaron was prepared for the difficulties. Like other black players traveling in the South, he knew he would not be allowed to stay in the same hotel as his white teammates and might some-times have to be lodged in the home of a black family. But on the field, Henry Aaron had few problems.

Years later, Aaron explained his method for dealing with racial prejudice. "There's only one way to break the color line," he said. "Be good. I mean, play good. Play so good that they can't remember what color you were before the season started."

Aaron played better than "good" for Jackson-ville. He batted a league-leading .362 with 208 hits and 125 RBIs. His performance earned him the Sally League's Most Valuable Player Award.

That same season, he met a young woman named Barbara Lucas who lived near the ballpark. She started attending some of the games, and Aaron took her to the movies on nights when he was free. Within a few months, the young couple became engaged. They were married shortly after the baseball season ended, on October 13, 1953.

During the winter of 1953–54, the Braves sent Aaron to play ball in Puerto Rico and learn to play the outfield. Although he was invited to

the Braves' spring training camp in Bradenton, Florida, he did not expect to make the major-league club that year. The Braves, who had finished in second place the year before, were expecting to make a run for the pennant. The team had just moved from Boston to Milwaukee, and its management was anxious to bring the new fans a championship. Toward that end, they had traded for Bobby Thomson, the Giants' veteran outfielder, to play left field and join sluggers Eddie Mathews, Joe Adcock, and Del Crandall in the batting order.

On March 13, however, in an exhibition game against the Yankees, Thomson broke his ankle sliding into third base. It turned out to be a big break for Aaron as well. The next day, Braves manager Charlie Grimm called Aaron aside and said, "Kid, you're my left fielder. It's yours until somebody takes it away from you." When Grimm

The young Henry Aaron with Ben Geraghty, his manager at Jacksonville. "I had a had a great friend and ally in Ben Geraghty," Aaron later said. "To this day, I believe that he was the best manager I ever played for. He taught me to study the game and never make the same mistake twice."

made that decision, he may have been influenced by a long home run Aaron had hit a few days earlier in Sarasota. The ball, which landed in a trailer park far beyond the left-field fence, could well have convinced the manager that the 20-year-old Aaron was ready to hit major-league pitching.

It soon became clear that Aaron was more than ready. After going hitless in his major-league debut in Cincinnati, he began to produce. His first homer came on April 23, off a future Hall of Famer, Robin Roberts. Roberts later commented that Aaron looked so relaxed at the plate he was the only batter who "could fall asleep between pitches and still wake up in time to hit the next one." Aaron's second home run came just two days later. He finished his rookie season with a respectable .280 batting average, 13 home runs, and 69 RBIs. These numbers might

Aaron watches the Braves' trainer examine his broken ankle. The September 5, 1954, injury probably cost Aaron a chance at Rookie of the Year honors.

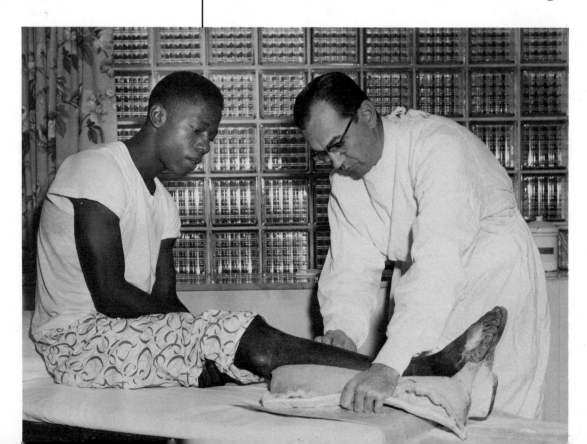

have been even higher had his season not ended early. On September 5, Aaron broke an ankle sliding into third base. As a result, he spent the remaining three weeks of the season on the bench. The Braves finished in third place, eight games behind the pennant-winning New York Giants.

Shortly after his rookie season had ended, Aaron set a goal for his sophomore year—to hit .300.

4

ALL-STAR AARON

Hank Aaron experienced his first banner season in 1955. Moved from left field to right field, where he would play during most of his career, he rapped out 189 hits and batted .314, fifth best in the National League. He scored 105 runs and drove in another 105. To top it off, he hit 27 homers and a league-leading 37 doubles. He also played in his first All-Star Game. Knocking in 100 runs or more and playing in the All-Star Game were going to become habits for Hammerin' Hank; he would drive in 100-plus runs 11 times and would play in the All-Star Game a remarkable 24 times (In the years 1959-1962, two All-Star games were played each year. Except for 1961, Aaron played in both games each year.)

Unfortunately, the Braves as a team did not do as well. Picked as a pennant contender in

Aaron, wearing number 5, slides into second base in 1954. Before the start of the 1955 season, he asked to wear a larger number and he was assigned number 44. Both the Brewers and the Braves retired number 44 when Henry stopped playing.

Aaron's speed, coordination, and throwing arm made him one of the best outfielders in baseball. He was named the top N.L. right fielder in three of the first four years the Gold Glove Award was given.

1955, they played inconsistently, far below their potential, and finished 13¹/₂ games behind the Brooklyn Dodgers.

Aaron was optimistic about the 1956 season, however. His manager, Charlie Grimm, was predicting an N.L. batting crown for his young right fielder. More important, the Braves still looked like sure contenders. Big Joe Adcock was set at first base; slugging Eddie Mathews was an All-Star third baseman; and Bill Bruton, the league's best base stealer, would be patroling center field. Best of all, the big three on the Braves' pitching staff—Warren Spahn, Lew Burdette, and Bob Buhl—were all potential 20-game winners.

Nevertheless, the Braves got off to a slow start. Through the first two months of the 1956 season, the team again played inconsistently. It would win two or three in a row, then lose two or three. By the middle of June, the Braves were barely over the .500 mark, while the aging Brooklyn Dodgers and surprising Cincinnati Reds were battling to lead the league.

On June 16, the Braves management fired Charlie Grimm and hired one of his coaches, Fred Haney, to manage the club. Inspired by their new leader, the Braves then blazed ahead with an 11-game winning streak that pushed them into first place. Spahn, Burdette, and Buhl became big winners, and Aaron went on a mid-summer 25-game hitting streak before being stopped by the Cardinals' Herm Wehmeier.

For the rest of the season, Milwaukee, Cincinnati, and Brooklyn leapfrogged each other in the standings, and the three-way contest continued past Labor Day. Going into the last weekend of the season, the Braves held a slim one-game lead over the Dodgers, with the Reds another game back, just waiting for their rivals to falter.

But on that final weekend, the Dodgers beat the Pirates three times, while the Braves lost two of three to the Cardinals, the last one a heart-breaking extra-inning battle between Spahn and Wehmeier. By Sunday night, the Braves were one game back, the Reds were two back, and the Dodgers were once more headed for the World Series.

Despite his team's failure on that final week-end, Aaron took some satisfaction in the 1956 season. As Charlie Grimm had predicted, Aaron had become the N.L.'s batting champ, with a .328 average. He also led the league with 200 hits and smacked out 26 homers. And he was again named to the National League All-Star team. It would have been a totally satisfying season for Aaron—if only his team had not lost those two big games at the end of the season. He hoped that 1957 would end differently—and it did.

CHAMPIONSHIP SEASONS

Fred Haney ran a tough spring training—pushing the Braves through endless exercise, drills, and sprints—to prepare his club for the long campaign. The hard work paid off immediately; the Braves burst into first place, winning 9 of their first 10 games. After that, however, the team again began to show the same inconsistency that had marked the two previous seasons. By mid-June, the Braves were 32–21, and the Reds were trailing by only 1 1/2 games.

On June 14, however, the Braves made a trade that would greatly affect the 1957 pennant race. They shipped the aging Bobby Thomson, second baseman Danny O'Connell, and a relief pitcher to the Cardinals for Red Schoendienst, a veteran second baseman. The steady Schoendienst was a fine fielder and a .300 hitter. Manager Haney immediately placed him second in the batting

Aaron is given a silver bat for winning the batting title in 1956. The following year, he led the league in homers, runs, and RBIs, and was leading in hitting until he sprained his ankle by stepping on a soda bottle that had been thrown on the field.

37

order, moving Aaron from that slot to the place where he could do the most good: cleanup.

Then, one month later, another valuable newcomer joined the club. Bob "Hurricane" Hazle was called up to Milwaukee from the Braves' farm team in Wichita, Kansas, when center fielder Bill Bruton injured his knee. Hazle lived up to his nickname with some whirlwind hitting—he finished the season with a remarkable .403 average in two months of play.

But in mid-September the Cardinals were still within striking distance of Milwaukee—only 2 1/2 games behind. This time, the Braves pulled together to meet the Cards' challenge with seven wins in a row. On Monday evening, September 23, the Braves were leading St. Louis by five games with only six left to play. Milwaukee was hosting St. Louis that night, so a victory would clinch the pennant for Aaron's club.

The Cardinals, led by the ageless Stan Musial, did not surrender easily. Three Card pitchers dueled Lew Burdette for 10 innings. The score was tied, 2–2, in the bottom of the 11th inning. With a runner on base and two outs, Aaron strolled to the plate to face a young reliever named Billy Muffett. Muffett threw Aaron a slow curveball that he blasted toward center field. The ball cleared the fence, and the Braves finally had their pennant!

Aaron's teammates mobbed him at the plate and carried him off the field. Years later, after he had broken Ruth's home-run record and reached so many other milestones, Aaron would still consider this homer—the 109th of his career—one of his greatest moments.

The Braves' World Series opponents were the powerful New York Yankees, who had easily run

After hitting a dramatic 11th-inning homer to give the Braves the 1957 pennant, Aaron is carried off the field. His homer came against Cardinal reliever Billy Muffett, who had not allowed a home run all season.

away with the American League pennant. The great Yankee players—including Mickey Mantle, Yogi Berra, Hank Bauer, and Whitey Ford—were used to pressure; they had appeared in seven of the previous eight World Series. Few of the Braves had ever played in a single championship game.

The Series opened at Yankee Stadium, with two stellar lefties, future Hall of Famers Warren Spahn and Whitey Ford, on the mound. Ford was the better man that day, limiting the Braves to five hits—one by Aaron—and winning, 3–1. The next day, it was Lew Burdette's turn to face the Yankees. The big right hander had won 20 games for the Braves and was now getting the chance to face the team with which he had started his major-league career in 1950. The Yankees of those years were deep with veteran pitchers and had dealt Burdette to the Braves. Now he was facing them for the first time. The score was tied, 2–2, in the 4th inning when the Braves got four hits and two runs off left-hander Bobby Shantz. Burdette hung on to win, 4–2. Aaron scored the game's first run after hitting a long triple over Mantle's head.

With the Series tied, 1–1, the action moved to Milwaukee. In game 3, the Yanks rolled over the Braves, 12–3, despite a homer by Aaron. In the fourth game, Aaron contributed a three-run homer to the Braves' 4–1 lead, but Elston Howard matched it with a three-run blast that tied the game in the 9th inning. The Yanks then scored another run in the top of the 10th, but Eddie Mathews gave the Braves, and Warren Spahn, a

Aaron chases a fly ball in the 1958 World Series, the second year in the row that the Braves and Yankees battled for the championship. Little did Aaron know that the 1958 Series would be his last.

7–5 victory with his three-run wallop in the bottom of the inning.

The Series was tied, 2–2, when Burdette took the mound for game 5. He pitched the game of his life, outdueling Ford and beating the Yanks, 1–0. Aaron was in the middle of the game's only rally: He pushed Mathews to second base with a single, which enabled him to score on Joe Adcock's hit.

Now the Braves needed only one more victory to become world champions, but that was easier said than done. New York's Bob Turley won game 6, 3–2, despite another homer by Aaron.

It was Burdette again in the seventh and deciding game. And again the Yanks could not touch him. He pitched a 7-hit shutout, and the Braves won, 5–0. Burdette, with his three victories, was undoubtedly the star of the Series, but Aaron finished the Series with a .393 average, 3 homers, and 7 RBIs.

At last, Hammerin' Hank was satisfied. Not only was he a member of a world championship team, but his individual stats were outstanding: He produced league-leading figures in homers (44) and RBIs (132) and a .322 average, third best in the National League behind Musial and Willie Mays. Aaron might have led the league in hitting as well had he not stepped on a soda bottle that had been thrown on the field by a fan. This slowed Aaron, and he blamed it for the drop in his hitting. For his great work in 1957, Aaron received the N.L.'s Most Valuable Player Award.

The year's end, however, brought a bittersweet event: Barbara Aaron gave birth to twin boys, one of whom died a few days later.

As 1958 began, Aaron looked forward to another great season. Not yet 24 years old, he was already one of the game's best players. And he was part of a team that seemed likely to repeat as National League champions.

The Braves did repeat in 1958, despite a slew of injuries that knocked some key players out of the lineup. Spahn won 22 games, and Burdette won another 20. Mathews, Frank Torre, and Wes Covington all turned in good seasons. And even though Aaron's RBI total dipped to 95, he still collected 30 homers while batting .326.

Once again, the Braves faced the Yanks in the World Series. This time it looked as though Milwaukee would easily eliminate its rivals. Behind Spahn and Burdette, the Braves won three of the first four games. But Burdette faltered in game 5, and three Yankee relief pitchers combined to beat Spahn, 4–3, in game 6. Burdette tried again in the final game, but the Yankee hitters got to him in the 8th inning, scoring 4 runs to break a 2–2 tie, and New York won the 1958 World Series.

Disappointed as he was, Aaron could not feel bad about his own play. Although he did not hit any home runs, he batted .333 in the Series. Besides, the 24-year-old slugger figured to play in several more Fall Classics before his career ended. As it turned out, however, the 1958 Series would be his last.

The Braves were contenders again in 1959. Although they played inconsistently for most of the season, they won 15 of their last 21 games to earn a first-place tie with the Dodgers, who had moved from Brooklyn to Los Angeles in 1957. In the best-of-three-games playoff at the end of the season, the Dodgers beat the Braves two straight to win the National League pennant.

Despite their team's disappointing finish,

Braves fans did not forget Aaron's outstanding season. He led the National League in batting with a .355 average and in hits with 223. He also hit 39 homers and drove in 123 runs. It looked like another MVP season for Aaron; but the award went to Ernie Banks of the Chicago Cubs, who hit 45 homers and drove in 143 runs.

After 1959, the Braves began a steady slide in the standings. They finished second in 1960, fourth in 1961, fifth in 1962, and sixth in 1963. In 1966, after two straight fifth-place finishes and a slip in home attendance, the team moved to Atlanta. These were not Aaron's happiest seasons; a player with his talents never enjoys playing for a noncontending team. But there was at least one bright spot for Aaron during that period. In 1962, the Braves signed his younger brother, Tommie, to a major-league contract. Tommie Aaron played with the Braves for parts of seven seasons, providing Hank with some companionship during losing campaigns. Tommie would later manage in the minors and coach with the Braves before dying of leukemia in 1984 at the age of 45.

Even as the club was floundering, Henry Aaron continued to play excellent ball. His average hovered around the .300 mark, and in 1963 and 1966, he won the National League home-run title and led the league in RBIs.

6

THE RACE

By the beginning of the 1967 baseball season, no one doubted that Henry Aaron would one day be elected to the Hall of Fame. He had already hit more than 400 home runs and was a sure bet to reach 500, a mark achieved by only a handful of players. His lifetime batting average was above .300, and he was not far away from 3,000 career hits, another milestone few players ever reach.

Aaron's success on the ball field could be attributed in part to natural talent. He was blessed with great speed and powerful arms and wrists. The great speed turned singles into doubles and accounted for his many stolen bases.

But Aaron also worked hard. From the moment he got to the ballpark, he was all business. "On the day of a night game I begin concentrating

Hank Aaron records his 3,000th career hit, against Cincinnati's Wayne Simpson. When Aaron was asked by a young fan if he ever broke a bat hitting, he replied, "I don't break bats, son, I wear them out."

at four in the afternoon," he once said. While waiting to bat in the on-deck circle, Aaron would study the man on the mound. He would remove his baseball cap and stare through one of the small holes on top to get a "close-up" view of the pitcher's delivery and release. If one of his children, sitting in a field-level box seat, happened to wave at him then, Aaron would be unlikely to notice.

When he stepped up to the plate, Aaron maintained his fierce concentration. Even when he hit a ball that was sure to leave the park, he would run all-out toward first base; he never paused to admire the blast. "My job is to get down to first base and touch it," he said. "Looking at the ball going over the fence isn't going to help."

It was this kind of attitude that made Aaron great. As far as his fans were concerned, there was nothing he could not do. But as the 1967

Atlanta-Fulton County Stadium, built in just 10 months, was opened for the 1966 season. Aaron did not hit the stadium's first homer—but he did steal the first base. During his career, Aaron hit more home runs in Atlanta than on the road, the reverse of his totals when he played in Milwaukee.

season began, few believed he would go after Babe Ruth's career home-run record of 714. Aaron had 442 homers at the time, but he was already 33 years old. Even Aaron did not think of himself as a true slugger. "I don't ever go up there swinging for home runs," he once told a reporter. "I swing to meet the ball. I want a base hit. If it goes out of the park, then I got a real good base hit. If it goes over the bag at second base, I got me a real good single."

And yet the home runs kept coming. Atlanta-Fulton County Stadium, where the Braves played their home games, was very friendly to home-run hitters. The ball traveled well there. In 1966, the Braves' first season in Atlanta, Aaron collected a league-leading 44 home runs. He led the league again in 1967 with 39; the following season, on July 14, he hit the 500th homer of his career. Still, a challenge to the Babe seemed quite unlikely. Aaron was now 34 years old, and he was still more than 200 homers shy of Ruth's total. Then he finished the 1968 season with only 29 homers, his lowest number in five seasons. Could it be that age was finally catching up to Hammerin' Hank?

Aaron answered that question with an outstanding 1969 season. He hit 44 four-baggers, batted .300 for the 12th time, scored 100 runs, drove in 97 runs, and led the league in total bases.

As a team, the Braves had a super season, too. After not contending for almost 10 years, they suddenly found themselves in a hot pennant race. The National League had just been divided into two divisions—Eastern and Western—and the Braves and the San Francisco Giants battled for the Western flag all season long. Behind Aaron's big bat, the Braves finally topped the

Giants in September and won their division by three games. Then they prepared to play a best-of-five series against the Eastern Division winners, the surprising New York Mets, for a chance to meet the American League champs in the World Series.

Mets pitchers Tom Seaver, Jerry Koosman, and Nolan Ryan were among the best in baseball, but the playoffs somehow turned into a slugfest. Though not noted for their hitting, the Mets pounded the Brave pitchers and won the series in three straight games: 9–5, 11–6, and 7–4. The defeat was hardly Aaron's fault. He homered in each of the three games, batted .357, and drove in 7 runs. Yet once again he was denied a shot at another world championship.

The following season, Aaron reached another important milestone. On May 17, 1970, he beat out a bouncer against the Reds' Wayne Simpson. The single was his 3,000th career hit. Only seven players in major-league history had done that before Aaron: Ty Cobb, Honus Wagner, Eddie Collins, Nap Lajoie, Tris Speaker, Paul Waner, and Stan Musial. As Aaron crossed the bag at Cincinnati's Crosley Field, a man jumped from his seat and raced across the field to congratulate Aaron on his achievement. It was Stan Musial, the only living Hall of Fame member with 3,000 hits. "It was getting awfully lonely," Musial said. "Congratulations, Henry." With Musial watching him, Aaron cracked a home run in his next at bat. It was number 570 on the road toward the Babe's 714 career home runs. And though the Braves slipped from contention in 1970, Aaron hit 38 home runs and drove in 118 runs.

By the end of the 1970 season, baseball fans

were finally beginning to believe the unbelievable: With his grand total of 592, Aaron had an outside shot at breaking Ruth's record. He had averaged better than 30 home runs a season over the previous five. But could he keep up that pace for four more seasons?

"This year and next year are going to be critical ones if I'm going to catch Babe Ruth," Aaron said at the start of the 1971 campaign. "I'd almost have to hit 50 in one of those seasons, I think. I'd need one big year, I know that."

The 1971 season would be a critical one for Hank on a personal level too. His marriage to Barbara Aaron had gradually come apart, and the two were divorced that winter. Aaron worried about the effect the breakup would have on their four children and the role he would play in their lives now that he was no longer married to their mother. To keep from dwelling on his family

After his 3,000th hit, Aaron (center) is congratulated by Braves owner Bill Bartholomay (right) and Stan Musial (left). Aaron later wrote, "I was proud to be joining a man I admired so much and pleased to carry on his tradition. Musial's hit number 3,001 was a homer and so was mine."

problems, he put all his energies into baseball.

And what a year 1971 turned out to be. The 37-year-old Aaron put together one of his very best seasons. Playing first base occasionally to rest his legs, and taking a day off when the Braves' schedule got too hectic, he hit 8 home runs in April and never stopped hitting them. That eighth April homer was a big one—his 600th lifetime round-tripper. Only Ruth and Willie Mays had more. Aaron did not hit 50 homers in 1971, but he came close with 47—the highest single-season total of his career. He also batted .327 and drove in 118 runs. When the season ended, he had 639 career homers. Baseball fans now knew it would be only a matter of time until Hank passed the Babe.

Aaron did not disappoint his fans. He stayed in shape and continued to play productively. His average dropped to .265 in 1972, but he hit 34 more homers, bringing his total to 673. He also passed Willie Mays that summer, leaving only the Babe ahead. Mays's career was coming to a close, but Aaron was still playing like a man in his prime.

In 1973, at age 39, Aaron again batted over .300. In fewer than 400 at bats—he was resting more frequently now —he hit 40 homers and had 96 RBIs. In September, when older players tend to tire, Aaron homered 7 times. His 713th came on September 29. He now trailed Ruth by only one.

September 30 was the last day of the season, and though the Braves were in sixth place in the National League West 40,000 fans showed up in Atlanta to see if Aaron could tie or top the Babe. But it was not to be. Although he rapped three singles to push his average to .301, his 16th .300 season, the big homer eluded him. He ended the season with 40 home runs, but he would have to wait until next year to become baseball's all-time home-run king.

Although most fans were rooting for Aaron to shatter Ruth's record, some did not want to see the Babe surpassed by anyone. Aaron himself seemed slightly uncomfortable with the inevitable comparisons. "Babe Ruth will still be the best, even if I pass him," he said. "Even if I'm lucky enough to hit 715 home runs, he will still be known as the greatest home-run hitter who ever lived."

Aaron also believed that all baseball fans had the right to root for or against whatever team or player they chose, so he was not upset when he heard fans say they wanted the Babe to remain on top. He was not inclined to take it personally, especially after speaking to Roger Maris, the Yankee slugger who broke Ruth's single-season

Aaron and teammates Darrell Evans (left) and Davey Johnson (right) each hit 40 or more home runs in 1973, the only time in baseball history three teammates reached that plateau in the same season.

home-run record in 1961. Maris had experienced some of the same treatment.

What did upset Aaron, however, were some letters he received from fans who were rooting against him. Aaron had thought that racism was, for the most part, a thing of the past in baseball. Considerably more upsetting were death threats made against Hank and his children. His daughter Gaile, who was attending college in Nashville, Tennessee, began getting strange phone calls and had to be kept under police surveillance for a time.

Fortunately, the threats proved to be empty. Aaron reacted to them with courage and dignity. "All I want is to be treated like a human being," he told reporters who asked him about the threats. "I've said it until it's tiresome: I'm not trying to be another Babe Ruth. All I'm trying to do is play the game and earn a living and be a part of my team." Then he added, "But I'll tell any fan this much: This kind of abuse isn't going to stop me. The more they push me, the more I want the record."

But the record was by no means the only thing on Aaron's mind. A year or so earlier, after appearing on an Atlanta television show, he had become friends with the show's hostess, Billye Williams. A widow in her mid-thirties, Williams had started a career in television after leaving her position as an English teacher at nearby Morris Brown College. The two became engaged during the summer of 1973, got married in Jamaica on November 12, and then spent a happy and relaxing off-season as newlyweds.

When the Braves' 1974 season opened in Cincinnati, Aaron was ready to resume his quest for the home-run record. But the Braves had another idea in mind: They wanted him to sit out the first series so that he would not hit his record-breaking home run on the road. But after sitting all winter, Aaron did not want to start the season on the bench. Neither did baseball Commissioner Bowie Kuhn, who stepped in and ordered the Braves to play Aaron in the season opener.

No one who had followed Aaron's career closely could have been surprised to see him take care of business so quickly after the season opened. After tying the Babe in his first at bat of the season in Cincinnati, he wanted to set the new record at home in front of his Atlanta fans. And that is exactly what he did. Number 715 came on his first swing in his first home game.

The rest of the season was somewhat anticlimactic for Aaron and his fans. At age 40, he appeared in just 112 games, batting only .268 with 20 homers. He considered retiring after the season but allowed the Braves to send him back to Milwaukee in a trade with the Brewers. Eager to play before the Milwaukee fans who had supported him so enthusiastically when the Braves played there, Aaron looked forward to a few more good seasons before ending his career.

THE FINAL SEASONS

Back in a Milwaukee uniform, Aaron signs autographs. Bud Selig, owner of the expansion Brewers, said, "There was nothing I was more proud of than bringing Hank Aaron back to Milwaukee, and that included giving the town a new franchise."

Aaron's last two seasons with the Brewers were not good ones. He was glad to be back in Milwaukee, and the fans were glad to have him. But this was not the Hank Aaron they remembered. At age 41, he found it difficult to learn a new league, and the American League pitchers kept him off balance. Used almost exclusively as a designated hitter, Aaron batted only .234 and .229 in his two Brewer seasons. Still, he was named to the All-Star team in 1975 for the 24th time, although it was his first time as an American Leaguer.

Aaron did have one great moment with the Brewers, however. In 1975, he erased Babe Ruth's lifetime mark of 2,211 runs batted in, and he eventually collected 2,297. He also wound up tied for second with Ruth in lifetime runs scored (2,174), and his hit total (3,771) placed him second on the all-time list behind Ty Cobb. Several years later, however, Pete Rose would pass both Aaron and Cobb in that department.

Aaron was as impressed with his hit total as he was with his home runs. "I look back now and 700 home runs look like a lot of home runs, and it is a lot of home runs," he said later. "I realize that I'm the only player who has made it besides Babe Ruth, too. But to make 3,000 base hits you have to be mighty consistent. In order to accomplish anything you have to hit the ball first."

But Aaron's long career owed as much to brilliance as it did to consistency. Both those qualities are acknowledged over and over again in baseball's record books. But perhaps the best testimony to Aaron's greatness came from two of his contemporaries. Mickey Mantle, the great Yankee center fielder, once said, "Aaron was to my time what Joe DiMaggio was to the era when he played." By comparing Aaron to DiMaggio, Mantle was stressing Aaron's superb command of all facets of the game: hitting for high average as well as for power, baserunning, and fielding. Like DiMaggio, Aaron did all those things splendidly.

Another home-run slugger, Reggie Jackson, who broke in in 1967 and went on to hit 563 career homers of his own, was in awe of Aaron's achievement. After hitting his 500th home run in 1984, Jackson was asked by a reporter how far up the lifetime home-run ladder he thought he might climb. Jackson allowed that he could most likely top Mantle's 536, but he just shook his head when the reporter mentioned Aaron's name. "If you hit 35 a year for 20 years," said Jackson, considering Aaron's total, "you're still 55 short."

In 1976, Aaron retired with a grand total of 755 home runs. But after 23 years in the majors, he still was not finished with baseball. He considered coaching and managing because he wanted to stay in uniform. "No indoor stuff for me," he declared. "No front office."

But in December 1976, the Atlanta Braves

coaxed Aaron to return to the team and work in the area of player development. There he rose to the rank of vice president and director of player development. And in December 1989, the man who had wanted no part of a front-office job was promoted to senior vice president and assistant to the president, which made him the highest-ranking black official in major-league baseball. He also does community-relations work for the Braves in the Atlanta area, where he lives.

Aaron's home-run days were over, the magic number, 755, inscribed in the record book. But there was still one honor yet to come. Five years after his retirement, the first year in which he was eligible for election into the Baseball Hall of Fame, Aaron was voted in by an overwhelming majority of the electors.

In August 1982, Henry Aaron was officially inducted into the Hall of Fame, along with Frank Robinson, who had played against him for many seasons. In his induction speech, Aaron made a point of thanking the great players who had paved the way for a black Alabama youngster to play big-league baseball.

"I'm proud to be standing where Jackie Robinson, Roy Campanella, and others made it possible for players like Frank Robinson and myself to prove that a man's ability is limited only by his lack of opportunity," he said.

It was typical of Aaron to remind fans of the achievements of those great players who had come before him. But he also had the right to be proud of his own accomplishments, several of which only two or three players have equaled, and one—his lifetime home-run record—that may well never be matched.

CHRONOLOGY

Feb. 5, 1934	Hank Aaron is born in Mobile, Alabama
Oct. 13, 1953	Marries Barbara Lucas of Jacksonville
March 1954	Becomes the left fielder of the Braves
1956	Wins his first N.L. batting title
Sept. 23, 1957	Belts 11th-inning homer to give Milwaukee the N.L. pennant
Nov. 1957	Named National League's Most Valuable Player
1958	The Braves win another pennant, but the Yankees win the Series
1959	Aaron wins another N.L. batting title, with a .355 average
1966	The Braves move to Atlanta; Aaron leads the National League with 44 homers
1967	Wins his fourth N.L. home-run title
May 17, 1970	Compiles his 3,000th career hit
Dec. 1970	Divorced from Barbara
Nov. 12, 1973	Marries Billye Williams of Atlanta
April 8, 1974	Hits his 715th homer, setting a new major-league home-run record
1975	Traded to the Milwaukee Brewers
Dec. 1976	Joins the Braves to work in player development
Aug. 1982	Inducted into the Baseball Hall of Fame

HENRY "HANK" L. AARON
MILWAUKEE N.L., ATLANTA N.L., MILWAUKEE A.L., 1954-1976

HIT 755 HOME RUNS IN 23-YEAR CAREER TO BECOME MAJORS' ALL-TIME HOMER KING. HAD 20 OR MORE FOR 20 CONSECUTIVE YEARS, AT LEAST 30 IN 15 SEASONS AND 40 OR BETTER EIGHT TIMES. ALSO SET RECORDS FOR GAMES PLAYED (3,298), AT-BATS (12,364), LONG HITS (1,477), TOTAL BASES (6,856), RUNS BATTED IN (2,297). PACED N.L. IN BATTING TWICE AND HOMERS, RUNS BATTED IN AND SLUGGING PCT. FOUR TIMES EACH. WON MOST VALUABLE PLAYER AWARD IN N.L. IN 1957.

MAJOR LEAGUE STATISTICS

MILWAUKEE BRAVES, ATLANTA BRAVES, MILWAUKEE BREWERS

YEAR	TEAM	G	AB	R	H	2B	3B	HR	RBI	BA	SB
1954	MIL N	122	468	58	131	27	6	13	69	.280	2
1955		153	602	105	189	37	9	27	106	.314	3
1956		153	609	106	200	34	14	26	92	.328	2
1957		151	615	118	198	27	6	44	132	.322	1
1958		153	601	109	196	34	4	30	95	.326	4
1959		154	629	116	223	46	7	39	123	.355	8
1960		153	590	102	172	20	11	40	126	.292	16
1961		155	603	115	197	39	10	34	120	.327	21
1962		156	592	127	191	28	6	45	128	.323	15
1963		161	631	121	201	29	4	44	130	.319	31
1964		145	570	103	187	30	2	24	95	.328	22
1965		150	570	109	181	40	1	32	89	.318	24
1966	ATL N	158	603	117	168	23	1	44	127	.279	21
1967		155	600	113	184	37	3	39	109	.307	17
1968		160	606	84	174	33	4	29	86	.287	28
1969		147	547	100	164	30	3	44	97	.300	9
1970		150	516	103	154	26	1	38	118	.298	9
1971		139	495	95	162	22	3	47	118	.327	1
1972		129	449	75	119	10	0	34	77	.265	4
1973		120	392	84	118	12	1	40	96	.301	1
1974		112	340	47	91	16	0	20	69	.268	1
1975	MIL A	137	465	45	109	16	2	12	60	.234	0
1976		85	271	22	62	8	0	10	35	.229	0
Totals		3298	12364	2174	3771	624	98	755	2297	.305	240
League Championship Series											
(1 year)		3	14	3	5	2	0	3	7	.357	0
World Series											
(2 years)		14	55	8	20	2	1	3	9	.364	0
All-Star Games											
(21 years)		24	67	7	13	0	0	2	8	.194	2

FURTHER READING

Aaron, Henry, with Furman Bisher. *Aaron.* New York: Crowell, 1974.

Aaron, Hank, with Lonnie Wheeler. *I Had a Hammer: The Hank Aaron Story.* New York: HarperCollins, 1991.

Ashe, Arthur T. *A Hard Road to Glory: A History of the African American Athlete.* Vol. 3. New York: Warner, 1988.

Baldwin, Stan, and Jerry Jenkins, in collaboration with Henry Aaron. *Bad Henry.* Radnor, PA: Chilton, 1974.

Charlton, James. *The Baseball Chronology.* New York: Macmillan, 1991.

Daley, Arthur. *All The Home Run Kings.* New York: Putnam, 1973.

Hahn, James, and Lynn Hahn. *Henry: The Sports Career of Henry Aaron.* Mankato, MN: Crestwood, 1981.

Musick, Phil. *Hank Aaron: The Man Who Beat the Babe.* New York: Popular Library, 1974.

Plimpton, George. *One for the Record: The Inside Story of Hank Aaron's Chase for the Home-Run Record.* New York: HarperCollins, 1974.

Sullivan, George. *Henry Aaron.* New York: Putnam, 1975.

Tygiel, Jules. *Baseball's Great Experiment: Jackie Robinson and His Legacy.* New York: Oxford University Press, 1983.

Voigt, David Q. *American Baseball.* Vol. 3. University Park: Pennsylvania State University Press, 1983.

INDEX

Page numbers in italics refer to illustrations.

PICTURE CREDITS

AP/Wide World Photos: pp. 20, 30, 34, 36, 39, 58; Atlanta Braves: pp. 2, 8, 46; *Eau Claire Leader-Telegram*, Eau Claire, WI: p. 22; National Baseball Library, Cooperstown, NY: pp. 12, 49, 51, 55, 60; UPI/Bettmann: pp. 11, 18, 25, 27, 29, 32, 40, 44; University of South Alabama Archives, Erik Overbey Collection: pp. 14, 17

JAMES TACKACH teaches in the Humanities Division at Roger Williams College in Bristol, Rhode Island. He is co-author of *Great Athletes of the 20th Century*, and his articles have appeared in the *New York Times*, *The Providence Journal*, *Sports History*, and a variety of academic journals. He lives in Narragansett, Rhode Island.

JIM MURRAY, veteran sports columnist of the *Los Angeles Times*, is one of America's most acclaimed writers. He has been named "America's Best Sportswriter" by the National Association of Sportscasters and Sportswriters 14 times, was awarded the Red Smith Award, and was twice winner of the National Headliner Award. In addition, he was awarded the J. G. Taylor Spink Award in 1987 for "meritorious contributions to baseball writing." With this award came his 1988 induction into the National Baseball Hall of Fame in Cooperstown, New York. In 1990, Jim Murray was awarded the Pulitzer Prize for Commentary.

EARL WEAVER is the winningest manager in Baltimore Orioles history by a wide margin. He compiled 1,480 victories in his 17 years at the helm. After managing eight different minor league teams, he was given the chance to lead the Orioles in 1968. Under his leadership the Orioles finished lower than second place in the American League East only four times in 17 years. One of only 12 managers in big league history to have managed in four or more World Series, Earl was named Manager of the Year in 1979. The popular Weaver had his number 5 retired in 1982, joining Brooks Robinson, Frank Robinson, and Jim Palmer, whose numbers were retired previously. Earl Weaver continues his association with the professional baseball scene by writing, broadcasting, and coaching.